THE

THREE

V'S

OF

SOCIETY

~by~

Marinus John William

Brønnum Rix Njelsen

Pedersen Cameron Tahu

(Friday, April 22, 2011)

THE CURTAIN OPENS

What follows is an observation of what I believe occurred, not an exemplification of what I believe should be; and as a man and a person it pains me that things were that way, but hopefully something can be learnt from the past to create a better future.

A

WOMANS

PLACE

TO

BEND

Yes, Helen is a villain, in that she stepped out of her appointed place in Greece – first in that she is a women and should remain unspoken of in good deeds and bad, and keep to her house – second in that she should have dressed modestly in mourning clothes when she was set to be a war spoil of Paris – thirdly she should have spoken only in reply after her accuser.

But only after, she was a victim of

her time and place, which

according to that time and place

duly men beneath gods and

women beneath men. But she also

was the result of the society that

molded her that way, where

women are silent as shades keep to

their houses though as men like

bats from the tree above the

entrance to the underworld flit

from the outside world of

commerce and combat.

Helen of Troy, born as a child of

her time and father Zeus, first

inspires a possible truce after Paris

and Menelaus hack it out in man-

on-man combat. Then later she

infuriates the other women by

embracing her victim hood and

thus transcending into a victor

when she dresses for her coming

wedding to her future husband

rather than to mourn for her old

husband.

A

MANS

PLACE

TO

RULE

The misogynist attitude to the

order of worth placed upon beings

in the Greek world where

appearance defines beauty, and

men can follow there lusts but re-

assign them as the will of the

Gods is seen in the following two

quotations:

"Paris, appalling Paris! Our prince

of beauty—mad for women, you

lure them all to ruin (Homer

128)." And "—Unholy, blind with

lust for gold—in secret now

catches Dido's husband off his

guard and cuts him down by

sword before the altars …

invented many stories to mock

Dido (Virgil 13)."

Men of Greece wanted their

women to be led by their mastery,

and they molded women to fit that

role, so when Helen left with Paris

for whatever motive she was

fulfilling that destiny – be it for

love, the sway of the gods, or whatever. It just didn't fit with what society deemed was her place, even though women are supposed to follow men unquestionably Greece, like many cultures has conflicting roles depending on what those above deem you should be doing. Men want women who can mange a household in their absence yet cry foul when a women points out that

the state is indeed a greater

household as translated by

Douglas Parker, and performed by

the Montford Park Players in the

Asheville Masonic Temple,

Asheville, North Carolina.

WOMEN

AS

THINGS

Men select to conquer women like

Athens seeks to conquer Sicily,

which they say as their job—

subdue all resistance to their

superiority, like the force taken

against Melos in the summer of

415.

They speak of women as property

not persons when they describe

woman by saying "Ah, no wonder

the men of Troy and Argive under

arms have suffered years of agony

all for her, for such a women.

Beautiful, terrible beauty! A

deathless goddess—so she strikes

the eyes" and "he keeps Helen

himself and all her wealth… the

Trojans surrender Helen and all

her treasures (Homer 13)."

Aeneas will carry his father on his

back while leading his son by his

hand yet does not realize his wife

is left behind until they are in a

safe place one wonders what place

his mother would be in if she were

alive.

"And the one who proves the

better man and wins, he'll take

those treasures fairly, and lead the

woman home. The rest will seal in

blood their binding pacts of

friendship (Homer 131)."

THE

WILL

OF

THE

GODS

In a society where a man far from

home can earn such an easy

marriage merely by sharing a cave

with a woman in rainstorm, and

desert her on the sway of the gods

there is a lot to say that men have

learnt their constancy from the

fickle gods while requiring women

to maintain constancy like the

Fates.

If Aeaneas could not resist leaving

Dido, with the excuse that the

gods were moving him, how could

Helen not use that same defense,

and be subject to it even more so

as women are supposed in that

time to be weaker than men?

The Penelopesian war 2.45

Pericles' speech to Athens state

funeral to the widow, and not

mothers – "subdue to your nature,

and be not spoken of either in

favor or ill – is your greatest

glory." Perhaps Helen is guilty of

doing something with her, rather than gliding through as a shade, in that they lack substance. "Power to the powerless – guilty of not being a pet of gods and men – like men are" (Euripides 20).

Helen rejecting love of Alexander / Paris is no more than a man who is stronger and smarter than women resisting the will of the Gods. They chose to be "beguiled by the sacred incantations &

therefore make their selves subject

to that. Sight engraves upon the

mind images of things that have

been seen.

And when this is how men treat

animals in service to their gods -

"he dragged the ruthless dagger

across the lambs' throats and let

them fall to the ground, dying,

grasping away … men said their

prayers to the gods who never die

(Homer 138)" – how can woman

who are also under the dominion

of men fare much better?

As Georgias notes "speech is a

powerful lord and men mold

women to follow them

unquestionably. The gods have a

stronger force than man has, in the

same was man has a stronger force

than women."

THE

FATES

"My Cythera, that's enough to fear; your children's fate is firm (Virgil 10)" is a conviction that the Fates hold the top rung in Greek society, even the gods have do deal with Fate. If only the Trojan Women could go to Thessaly and have the witches there teach them to turn back time and re-do their fates more acceptably. But the Fates will choose what they will; Even the

Gods have to accept that!

It was mans fault for not making

women their equals who would

have acted equally intelligently as

them had they been trained to by

society.

Greek society got what it wanted -

lesser beings being ruled by

greater beings – therefore Greek

society needs to look to their gods

of those who defined them – why did they not make everyone equals and avoid this tragedy?

The society that molded Helen as a victim rejected her as a villain for the same reason that I believe she is a victor – she became dangerous through becoming more than her society could tolerate her to be. She lived "long enough to become the villain (Batman, Dark Knight)."

Granted that is maybe some

women are as sly as men of today

desire, but wear the face of the

dominated, but even so you cannot

balance the sack of Troy on one

person's back whatever rank or

gender, like you cannot call it a

tricycle and only attach one wheel.

SOURCES

CITED

Aristophanes. Lysistrata. United
States: Free Dover, 2005. 1994.
Print.

Euripides. The Trojan Women.
United States: Penguin Books,
2005. 10. Print.

Euripides. The Trojan Women.

United States: Penguin Books,

2005. 20. Print.

Homer. The Iliad. New York, New

York: Penguin Books, 1991. 128.

Print.

Homer. The Iliad. New York, New

York: Penguin Books, 1991. 131.

Print.

Homer. The Iliad. New York, New
York: Penguin Books, 1991. 138.
Print.

Virgil. The Aeneid of Virgil. New
York, New York: Bantam Dell,
2004. 10 Print.

Virgil. The Aeneid of Virgil. New
York, New York: Bantam Dell,
2004. 13. Print.